The Royal Family

WILLIAM and KATE

ANNABEL SAVERY

WAYLAND
www.waylandbooks.co.uk

First published in Great Britain in 2018 by Wayland
Copyright © Hodder and Stoughton Limited, 2018

ISBN 978 1 5263 0627 2

10 9 8 7 6 5 4 3 2 1

Wayland
An imprint of
Hachette Children's Group
Part of Hodder & Stoughton
Carmelite House
50 Victoria Embankment
London EC4Y 0DZ
An Hachette UK Company
www.hachette.co.uk
www.hachettechildrens.co.uk

A catalogue for this title is available from the British Library.
Printed in China.

Produced for Wayland by
White-Thomson Publishing Ltd
www.wtpub.co.uk

Editor: Annabel Savery
Designer: Rocket Design (East Anglia Ltd)
In-house editor: Sarah Silver

Picture acknowledgements:
Alamy: 8 Pictorial Press Ltd/Alamy Stock Photo, 9b BRIAN HARRIS/Alamy Stock Photo; Getty Images:
Cover Samir Hussein/Contributor, 5 Chris Jackson/Staff, 6 Hulton Archive/Stringer, 7 Karwai Tang/Contributor,
10tr Ken Goff/Contributor, 12 Mark Cuthbert/Contributor, 15tr WPA Pool/Pool, 17 Handout/Handout,
18 Ian Gavan/GP/Contributor, 20 Samir Hussein/Contributor, 21t Handout/Handout, 21b Chris Jackson/
Staff, 23 Karwai Tang/Contributor, 24tl Pool/Samir Hussein/Contributor, 27b WPA Pool/Pool; iStockPhoto: 16t
csfotoimages; Shutterstock: 4 MediaPictures.pl, 9t mary416, 10bl Travel Stock, 11 Heidi Sevestre, 13 Gail Johnson,
14 luisrsphoto, 15b Michael Conrad, 16b Featureflash Photo Agency, 19 Featureflash Photo Agency, 22 & 30 Mr
Pics, 24br Nils Versemann, 25 Shaun Jeffers, 26tr Frederic Legrand – COMEO, 26bl Frederic Legrand - COMEO.
All graphic elements courtesy of Shutterstock.

CONTENTS

William and Kate

In April 2011, royal prince and heir to the throne, William, married his non-royal fiancée, Kate Middleton. Since then, the couple have started a family and Kate has learnt what royal life is like. We see thousands of press pictures of them as they visit charities, watch sporting and musical events, and attend official ceremonies.

ROYAL TALK

'We are looking forward to spending the rest of our lives together and seeing what the future holds.'

Prince William, talking about his engagement to Kate, 2010.

∧ William and Kate meet the President and First Lady of Poland on their visit there in June 2017.

Family life

William and Kate have three children, Prince George, Princess Charlotte and Prince Louis. They have homes in London and Norfolk, and own a cocker spaniel dog called Lupo. The couple spend their time carrying out royal duties and supporting charities and issues that they are passionate about. They are known as the Duke and Duchess of Cambridge, a title given to them by the Queen when they were married.

Three kings

Prince William is a member of the British royal family. The Queen is his grandmother. When his father, Prince Charles, becomes king, William will be next in line to the throne. After his father's reign, Prince George will become king. It's an important job, one that the Princes prepare for their whole lives.

The Duke and Duchess of Cambridge, with their children – Prince George and Princess Charlotte – at a children's play day during their visit to Canada in 2016.

∨

WILL & KATE FUN FACTS

William used to cook for Kate at university, but usually ended up burning something.

William proposed to Kate while they were on holiday in Kenya.

Kate is allergic to horses.

The couple enjoy a takeaway curry — but say it is a struggle to get it delivered to the palace.

William's royal family

The British royal family is made up of Queen Elizabeth II and her whole family. It is a family like any other, with mums, dads, grandparents, cousins, uncles and aunts. So why are they so important?

The Queen

Elizabeth II is Queen of England, Wales, Scotland and Northern Ireland, and 15 overseas territories. She has reigned since February 1952, which makes her the longest-ruling monarch in British history.

What does the Queen do?

The Queen is Head of State and the Head of the Church of England. It is the Queen's role to represent the UK both at home and abroad, and to host the heads of other states when they visit the UK. She leads ceremonial occasions, such as Remembrance Day, and celebrations, such as Trooping the Colour. The Queen is also a patron for many charities and associations. She spends her time reading state papers from the government and visiting schools, hospitals, charities and other places to show her support for them.

< Queen Elizabeth II was just 27 when she was crowned in 1953.

The immediate family

Princess Elizabeth Windsor married Philip Mountbatten, Prince of Greece and Denmark, in 1947. After their wedding, Philip gave up his Greek royal title and became Prince Philip, Duke of Edinburgh. The Queen and Prince Philip have four children: Charles, Anne, Andrew and Edward. They also have eight grandchildren (William is one of them) and six great-grandchildren. The role of the royal family is to support the Queen in her duties, and carry out public duties of their own.

The royal family stand on the balcony of Buckingham Palace to watch planes fly past, part of the Trooping the Colour celebration, 2017. ⌄

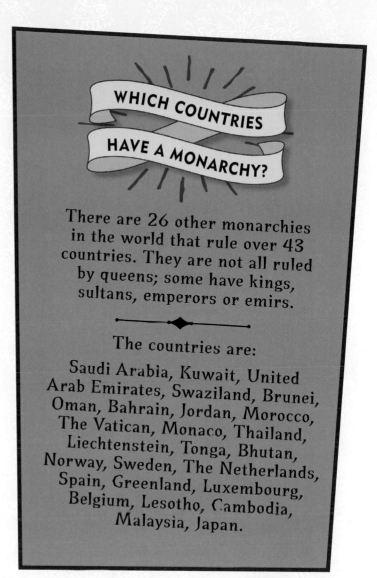

WHICH COUNTRIES HAVE A MONARCHY?

There are 26 other monarchies in the world that rule over 43 countries. They are not all ruled by queens; some have kings, sultans, emperors or emirs.

The countries are:

Saudi Arabia, Kuwait, United Arab Emirates, Swaziland, Brunei, Oman, Bahrain, Jordan, Morocco, The Vatican, Monaco, Thailand, Liechtenstein, Tonga, Bhutan, Norway, Sweden, The Netherlands, Spain, Greenland, Luxembourg, Belgium, Lesotho, Cambodia, Malaysia, Japan.

Early days

Prince William Arthur Philip Louis Windsor was born on 21 June 1982 at St Mary's Hospital, London. As is traditional for the royal family, his birth was announced by a notice placed inside the gates of Buckingham Palace.

A baby boy

William's parents, Charles and Diana, the Prince and Princess of Wales, were thrilled with the arrival of their baby boy. He was first shown to the public outside the hospital in London where Kate and William would stand with their son George, 31 years later.

Baby Prince William with his parents, the Prince and Princess of Wales, in December 1982.
∨

William lived at Kensington Palace when he was young and it is his family's London home today.

Family life

William's younger brother Harry was born on 15 September 1984. The family lived at Kensington Palace in London, but also had a countryside home. William and Harry were given as normal a childhood as possible with toys, games, and trips to the cinema and places such as Thorpe Park.

Off to school

When he was three, Charles and Diana took William to his first day at nursery school in London. Then, in 1990, when he was eight, he started boarding school. The school was made as home-like as possible, and he shared a dormitory with four other boys. There was a golf course and a swimming pool, and each boy had a tuck box full of treats to last the term.

Eton and tragedy

When he was thirteen, William started at Eton. It is a boys' private school and one of the oldest schools in the country. Two years later, in August 1997, Diana was killed in a car crash in Paris. The family were devastated.

ROYAL TALK

In 2017, William and Harry spoke publically about losing their mother at such a young age.

'We've been brought closer because of the circumstances. We know we are uniquely bonded because of what we've been through, but even Harry and I over the years have not talked enough about our mother.'

Prince William, from a video made for their mental health charity, Heads Together.

∧ William and Harry walked behind the coffin with their father, grandfather and uncle.

Growing up

Following the death of their mother, Prince Charles asked the media to leave the boys to have as normal a school life as possible. They would do scheduled photo shoots, but were not to be followed around.

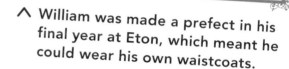

Finishing school

William returned to Eton and was joined by Harry in 1998. He passed 12 GCSEs and then chose geography, biology and history of art for his A-level subjects. He played lots of sports, including rugby, but particularly enjoyed swimming, and was captain of the water polo team.

∧ William was made a prefect in his final year at Eton, which meant he could wear his own waistcoats.

∨ William's time in Africa showed him the importance of wildlife conservation, an issue that he is still passionate about today.

A gap year

William decided to take a gap year before going to university. First, he went to Belize to train with the Welsh Guards army regiment and do some scuba diving. Then, he volunteered in Chile with the project Raleigh International. This organisation puts young volunteers to work on community projects around the world. There was no luxury – the Prince shared a tent and did the tough work with everyone else. For one project, his group helped villagers to build wooden walkways between their homes. William also visited Africa and spent time on a rhino reserve in Kenya.

∧ University buildings are spread through the town of St Andrews.

St Andrews

William chose the University of St Andrews, Scotland, for his degree. He was planning to study history of art but later switched to geography. He carried on with water polo at university, made new friends and went to parties along with everyone else. William graduated in 2005 with a 2:1 degree, and the Queen and Duke of Edinburgh attended the ceremony along with Prince Charles and Camilla, Duchess of Cornwall.

It was at St Andrews that William met Kate Middleton. She was also studying history of art and they were in the same halls for the first year. They became friends and along with two others, decided to share a house for their second year.

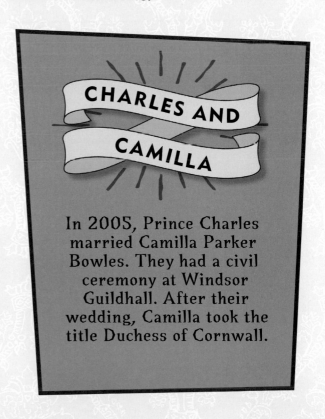

CHARLES AND CAMILLA

In 2005, Prince Charles married Camilla Parker Bowles. They had a civil ceremony at Windsor Guildhall. After their wedding, Camilla took the title Duchess of Cornwall.

Becoming a pilot

After university, William chose to follow royal tradition and undertake military training. The monarch is head of the armed forces, and as William will one day assume this role, it made sense that he should gain inside knowledge.

An officer cadet

William passed the first round of selection tests and, in 2006, began officer training at Sandhurst Royal Military Academy. Officer training is a tough course and William was treated the same as all the other recruits. Training takes 44 weeks and is made up of physical, practical, military and academic training. At the end, new officers 'Pass out' at the Sovereign's Parade. His father, Camilla, Kate and her family watched on.

In the forces

Although William wanted to serve on the front line, it was thought that it would be too dangerous. Being the heir to the throne, people were concerned that he would become a target for attack. It had been possible for his brother Harry to serve in secret, but only until his involvement became known by the media. Instead, William chose to train with the other divisions of the armed forces. He trained to pilot aircraft with the RAF and spent time on a destroyer with the Navy.

December 2006: > At the Sovereign's Parade, William was inspected by his grandmother the Queen.

ROYAL PILOTS

Prince Philip left the navy and trained as a pilot when Elizabeth became Queen.

◆

Prince Charles has a pilot's licence.

◆

Prince Andrew was a pilot during the Falkland's War.

◆

Prince William of Gloucester (the Queen's cousin) was a keen pilot but died when his light aircraft crashed during an air race.

Getting his wings

Next, William decided to continue with the armed forces and to train as a RAF search and rescue pilot. He was posted at RAF Valley in North Wales and spent three years based on the Island of Anglesey. The search-and-rescue team take on eight 24-hour shifts per month, plus training. William rented a cottage nearby and did his own cooking and shopping. Kate visited often and the couple enjoyed the peace and quiet of the island.

When on duty, Prince William is known as 'William Wales'.

A search-and-rescue Sea King helicopter on ❯ exercise in Anglesey. During his time with the search-and-rescue team, William took part in 156 operations with 149 people being rescued.

Young Kate

In the past, young royals have been expected to marry other royals. However, Kate is not a royal. She was born Catherine Elizabeth Middleton on 9 January 1982 at the Royal Berkshire Hospital.

Kate's family

Kate's parents, Michael and Carole, met when they were both working for the same airline. Carole was an air stewardess and Michael was a flight dispatcher. Kate has a younger sister, Pippa, and brother, James. When she was two, Kate's family moved to Amman in Jordan. When they returned to England in 1986, Carole started her own business from home called Party Pieces. Kate and Pippa helped out by modelling T-shirts for the catalogue.

Some members of Bucklebury village, where Kate grew up, were at William and Kate's wedding, including the butcher, postman and shopkeeper!

∨ Amman is the capital of Jordan. Kate's family had a one-storey apartment in the city.

Kate (front row, centre) with her school hockey team. Kate re-visited the school in 2012 and described her years there as 'some of her happiest'.

A new school

Kate had been to nursery in Jordan, and learnt nursery rhymes in Arabic. When the family returned from Jordan, it was time for her to start school. She attended St Andrew's school in Pangbourne, Berkshire. She was good at sports and held the record for the high-jump. Kate also enjoyed music: she was in the choir and played the flute in a group called the Tootie-Flooties!

Birthdays and Brownies

Unlike William's, Kate's childhood was quite ordinary. She started Brownies and went on camping trips with them. With her dad working for a big airline, foreign holidays were no problem, but the family also went camping and walking in the Lake District. The family loved to celebrate birthdays with themed parties and homemade cakes – Kate's favourite was a white marshmallow rabbit cake.

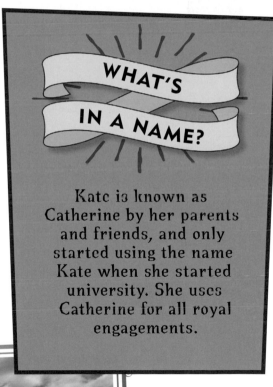

WHAT'S IN A NAME?

Kate is known as Catherine by her parents and friends, and only started using the name Kate when she started university. She uses Catherine for all royal engagements.

< Kate's family enjoyed exploring the Lake District.

What Kate did next

∧ Marlborough College opened in 1843 as a boys'
school, it has been open to boys and girls since 1989.

School days

Kate was originally enrolled in the Downe House school, which
was close to the family home. She wasn't happy there and moved
to Marlborough College, where she boarded. There was a strong
focus on sport in the school which suited her. Kate played hockey,
tennis, netball and became a prefect. She was able to travel too,
and went on a tour of Brazil and Argentina with the school
hockey team. Kate left Marlborough with A-levels in
chemistry, biology and art.

William's cousin Princess Eugenie >
also went to Marlborough College.

Another St Andrews

Like William, Kate had a gap year. She spent time studying Italian at the British Institute in Florence, and was also a volunteer with Raleigh International. She chose St Andrews University and the history of art course – having no idea she would be living with royalty. She graduated in 2005, on the same day as William, with a 2:1 degree.

> William and Kate on their graduation day, 23 June 2005.

Finding work

After university, Kate wasn't sure what she wanted to do next. Her degree didn't lead directly into a career so she tried out a few things. She had a flat in Chelsea, in London, and also spent time at her family home. Kate took on a role working as a buyer for the clothing company Jigsaw, and also worked for her parents' business. She is a keen photographer and took photos for the company. She also developed part of the business that focuses on first birthdays.

A tricky time

The years after university were tricky for Kate. She and William had become a couple at university but were now doing different things. His training with the military meant that they didn't see much of each other. She also had problems with the media, as journalists camped outside her front door and followed her around London. She and William split up briefly in 2007, but were soon back together and looking to the future.

The happy couple

After seven years together, William proposed in 2010 while the couple were on holiday in Kenya. Kate's engagement ring is a sapphire surrounded by diamonds that once belonged to William's mother, Diana.

The big day

William and Kate were married at Westminster Abbey on 29 April 2011. They had a traditional Christian service led by the Archbishop of Canterbury. There were 1,900 guests at the wedding, including friends and family, but also politicians, other royals and military personnel. Kate's father walked her down the aisle, and Prince Harry was best man.

∨ **Kate in her traditional long white dress, and Prince William in the uniform of an Irish Guards colonel.**

THAT DRESS!

Kate's wedding dress was kept a complete secret and those making it were sworn to secrecy. It was designed by Sarah Burton from the fashion house Alexander McQueen. Kate also wore a tiara lent to her by the Queen.

Celebrations

After the ceremony, William and Kate rode in an open top carriage to Buckingham Palace for a reception hosted by the Queen. They appeared on the balcony to a crowd of around 500,000 people, waved, smiled and shared a kiss. After the reception, the couple sped away from Buckingham Palace in an Aston Martin car lent to them by Prince Charles. It had been decorated by Harry with streamers and a 'Just Wed' number plate. Later, Prince Charles hosted a reception for 300 people at the palace with dinner and dancing.

The couple's wedding cake was made up of 17 fruit cakes. But they also had a chocolate biscuit cake requested by William!

The honeymoon

The couple had a weekend away after their big day, but William was back at work on Monday. They went on honeymoon later in the year and even managed to keep the destination a secret. People found out later that they enjoyed a break in the Seychelles.

ROYAL WEDDING IN NUMBERS

24.5 million — the number of people worldwide who watched the TV coverage.

One million — the number of people who lined the streets to watch the cars and carriages pass.

2.7 metres — the length of Kate's wedding dress train.

10,000 — the number of canapés served at the afternoon reception.

∧ The newlyweds waved to crowds as they drove through London after their wedding ceremony.

A family home

Before getting married, William and Kate split their time between peaceful Anglesey and bustling London. After the wedding, William continued to work for the search-and-rescue team and Kate began to think about what causes she would like to support in her new role.

Starting a family

In December 2012, it was announced that Kate was expecting a baby. She was taken to hospital early in the pregnancy with acute morning sickness, but soon returned home. George Alexander Louis was born in St Mary's Hospital, London, on 22 July 2013. The media waited outside the hospital for the first glimpse of the new prince. In September 2013, William's posting with the RAF was at an end and the family left Anglesey for Kensington Palace, in London.

William and Kate > show baby Prince George to the waiting media.

Moving again

William and Kate chose to spend their early years as a family at their countryside home, Anmer Hall, in Norfolk. In February 2015, William passed his Air Transport License, and in March he began working for the East Anglian Air Ambulance. Then, on 2 May 2015, Prince George's little sister arrived. She was named Princess Charlotte Elizabeth Diana.

Next steps

In 2017, the couple announced that William was to leave the Air Ambulance. William and Kate now focus on royal duties and are patrons of many organisations and charities. Their main home is in Kensington Palace. In September, they announced they were expecting again and on 23 April 2018 Prince Louis Arthur Charles was born.

∧ William and Kate with George and Charlotte at Kensington Palace, December 2015.

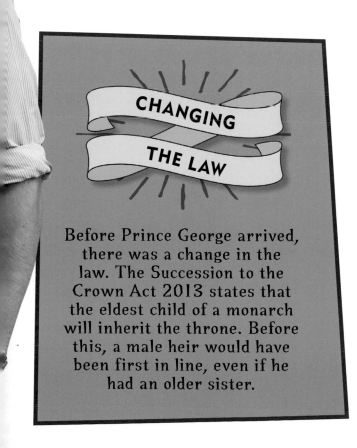

CHANGING THE LAW

Before Prince George arrived, there was a change in the law. The Succession to the Crown Act 2013 states that the eldest child of a monarch will inherit the throne. Before this, a male heir would have been first in line, even if he had an older sister.

∧ Kate shows Prince Louis to the world on the steps outside the hospital. He will be fifth in line to the throne.

Their work today

As well as raising their young family, the Duke and Duchess of Cambridge take on royal duties, both to support the Queen and to raise awareness of causes close to their hearts.

The Royal Foundation

When Princes William and Harry reached adulthood, they created a foundation to bring together organisations they support. When William and Kate married, the foundation became The Royal Foundation of The Duke and Duchess of Cambridge and Prince Harry. There are three main areas that the young royals focus on: the armed forces, young people and conservation.

⌄ Will, Kate and Harry at St Paul's Cathedral, June 2017.

> Tensions mount as England play Wales in the 2015 Rugby World Cup, and the royals watch on!

Time for sport

William and Kate have always been keen on sports and both played at school. William is president of The Football Association (FA). William is also president of The British Sub-Aqua Club, a patron of the English Schools' Swimming Association and patron of the Welsh Rugby Union. In 2017, Kate became patron of the All England Lawn Tennis and Croquet Club that hosts the annual Wimbledon tennis tournament.

Helping young people

When William was young, he visited many of his mother's charities with her. These visits made a lasting impression on the young prince and one of the first organisations he chose to support was the homeless charity Centrepoint. Although he makes official visits and gives speeches, he also makes it a priority to meet young people and talk about their problems. He has cooked breakfast for them and spent a night sleeping on the streets in -4°C temperatures to find out what their lives can be like.

Kate has also chosen to support charities that help young people. Following her marriage, one of the first charities she chose to support was Place2Be, a youth counselling service.

ROYAL TALK

'The visit I made as a child to this place left a deep and lasting impression upon me.'

Duke of Cambridge, 2016, talking about his visit to re-open a homeless shelter he first visited with his mother as a boy.

The royals abroad

Travel has always been part of royal life. These royal visits support relations between countries. When William and Kate travel abroad, they represent the Queen and the United Kingdom. Their visits usually include activities typical of the culture of the host nation.

The Commonwealth

Britain once had a large empire – a group of countries all ruled by the British government. Many of these countries are now independent nations that govern themselves. After their independence, they were still united as the British Commonwealth of Nations. Today, the Commonwealth is an association for nations that were once part of an empire. It has 52 member countries.

< The family arrive in Warsaw, Poland in 2017.

The Commonwealth Games is held every four years. This clock was used to count down the time until the 2018 games on Australia's Gold Coast. >

< William and Kate visited New Zealand on a royal tour in 2014. The couple took part in a yacht race, which Kate won!

Australia and New Zealand

In 1983, baby Prince William travelled with his parents on a six-week tour of Australia and New Zealand. He was just learning to crawl and stand up. In July 2005, William made his first official visit overseas when he went to New Zealand to represent the Queen on the 60th anniversary of the Second World War. In 2010 he visited again, this time as a tour, and he returned in 2011 after Australia and New Zealand were struck by an earthquake.

Canada

Following their wedding, William and Kate went on a royal tour of Canada. It was Kate's first royal tour and the young couple had a busy schedule. It included visits to seven cities, dragon boat racing, opening the annual Calgary Stampede, a visit to a cookery school, in addition to other official duties and receptions. In 2016 they visited Canada again, this time as a family. Prince George and Princess Charlotte made an appearance at a children's play day, with balloons, a petting zoo and miniature ponies.

HEAD OF STATE

The Queen is head of state of 15 kingdoms, as well as the UK. These are: Antigua and Barbuda, Australia, The Bahamas, Belize, Barbados, Canada, Grenada, Jamaica, New Zealand, Papua New Guinea, St Kitts and Nevis, St Lucia, St Vincent and the Grenadines, Solomon Islands and Tuvalu.

ROYAL TALK

'We feel very lucky to have been able to introduce George and Charlotte to Canada. This country will play a big part in the lives of our children.'

Prince William on his family visit to Canada in 2016.

A future king

After the Queen, Prince Charles will become king. Prince William will then become king after his father. When Charles becomes king, Prince William will become the Prince of Wales.

Prince Charles ⌄

< Prince William

A new Prince of Wales

When Prince Charles accedes to the throne, he will pass his title and the Duchy of Cornwall to his eldest son, Prince William. The duchy is a collection, or portfolio, of land and property owned by Prince Charles that provide his income. Kate will become Catherine Princess of Wales. She will not be 'Princess Catherine', as this is a title that you can only inherit by birth.

NAME CALLING

When Charles and William become kings, they can either choose to keep their first names and become King Charles III and King William V, or they can choose another name to be known by. The Queen's father was known as George VI but his first name was actually Albert.

Looking forward

In August 2017, at the age of 96, the Duke of Edinburgh retired from public duties. The Queen is also reducing the number of organisations that she is patron of, so now the younger royals are taking on more duties.

A big change

When William becomes king, it will mean a big change for the whole family. They may move to live in Buckingham Palace as the Queen and her family did. As the wife of a monarch, Kate will become Queen Catherine. George will become heir to the throne. To prepare for their role as senior royals, William and Kate will take on more royal duties and patronages, representing the Queen as they gain more experience of royal life.

∧ The Queen and Prince Philip attend Royal Ascot in 2015.

ROYAL TALK

'Speaking for myself, I am privileged to have the Queen as a model for a life of service to the public.'

Prince William, 2015, talks about taking his grandmother, the Queen, as a role model.

William and Kate now join the senior royals at important state occasions. Here, they gather for the Annual Diplomatic Corps Reception at Buckingham Palace in 2016. ∨

Kings and Queens of England

The House of Normandy

William I (*William the Conqueror*)	1066–1087
William II (*William Rufus*)	1087–1100
Henry I	1100–1135
Stephen	1135–1154

The House of Plantagenet

Henry II	1154–1189
Richard I (*Richard the Lionheart*)	1189–1199
John	1199–1216
Henry III	1216–1272
Edward I	1272–1307
Edward II	1307–1327
Edward III	1327–1377
Richard II	1377–1399

The House of Lancaster

Henry IV	1399–1413
Henry V	1413–1422
Henry VI	1422–1461

The House of York

Edward IV	1461–1483
Edward V	1483–1483
Richard III	1483–1485

The House of Tudor

Henry VII	1485–1509
Henry VIII	1509–1547
Edward VI	1547–1553
Jane	1553–1553
Mary I	1553–1558
Elizabeth I	1558–1603

The House of Stuart

James I (James VI of Scotland)	1603–1625
Charles I	1625–1649
Commonwealth declared	
Oliver Cromwell Lord Protector	1653–1658
Richard Cromwell Lord Protector	1658–1659
Monarchy restored	
Charles II	1649 (*restored 1660*)–1685
James II (*James VII of Scotland*)	1685–1688
William III and Mary II	1689–1694 (Mary)
	1702 (*William*)
Anne	1702–1714

The House of Hanover

George I	1714–1727
George II	1727–1760
George III	1760–1820
George IV	1820–1830
William IV	1830–1837
Victoria	1837–1901

The House of Saxe-Coburg – becomes House of Windsor in 1917

Edward VII	1901–1910
George V	1910–1936
Edward VIII (*abdicated*)	1936–1936
George VI	1936–1952
Elizabeth II	1952–

The royal family tree

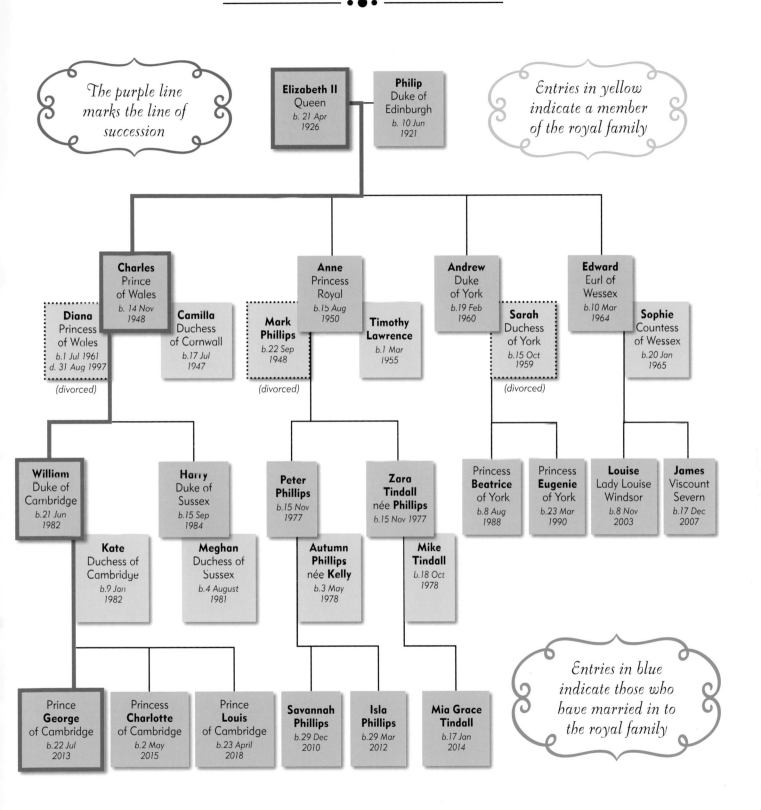

The purple line marks the line of succession

Entries in yellow indicate a member of the royal family

Elizabeth II Queen *b. 21 Apr 1926*

Philip Duke of Edinburgh *b. 10 Jun 1921*

Charles Prince of Wales *b. 14 Nov 1948*

Diana Princess of Wales *b.1 Jul 1961 d. 31 Aug 1997* (divorced)

Camilla Duchess of Cornwall *b.17 Jul 1947*

Anne Princess Royal *b.15 Aug 1950*

Mark Phillips *b.22 Sep 1948* (divorced)

Timothy Lawrence *b.1 Mar 1955*

Andrew Duke of York *b.19 Feb 1960*

Sarah Duchess of York *b.15 Oct 1959* (divorced)

Edward Earl of Wessex *b.10 Mar 1964*

Sophie Countess of Wessex *b.20 Jan 1965*

William Duke of Cambridge *b.21 Jun 1982*

Kate Duchess of Cambridge *b.9 Jan 1982*

Harry Duke of Sussex *b.15 Sep 1984*

Meghan Duchess of Sussex *b.4 August 1981*

Peter Phillips *b.15 Nov 1977*

Autumn Phillips née **Kelly** *b.3 May 1978*

Zara Tindall née **Phillips** *b.15 Nov 1977*

Mike Tindall *b.18 Oct 1978*

Princess **Beatrice** of York *b.8 Aug 1988*

Princess **Eugenie** of York *b.23 Mar 1990*

Louise Lady Louise Windsor *b.8 Nov 2003*

James Viscount Severn *b.17 Dec 2007*

Prince **George** of Cambridge *b.22 Jul 2013*

Princess **Charlotte** of Cambridge *b.2 May 2015*

Prince **Louis** of Cambridge *b.23 April 2018*

Savannah Phillips *b.29 Dec 2010*

Isla Phillips *b.29 Mar 2012*

Mia Grace Tindall *b.17 Jan 2014*

Entries in blue indicate those who have married in to the royal family

Glossary

abdicate when the heir to the throne steps down and refuses the position

accede to take up a position

conservation work and programmes that protect animals and environments

destroyer a small, fast warship in the Royal Navy

empire a collection of countries reigned over by a single monarch or state

graduate to complete a university degree or other course

halls (of residence) accommodation for students at university, usually in the first year

legacy something that a person leaves behind after they die

patron a person who supports an organisation or charity

Remembrance Day 11 November; this day marks the end of the First World War and each year a service is held to remember those who died

scuba diving a sport where people use breathing equipment to swim deep underwater

succession to inherit a title or role, or the line of those who will take up a role or title

Trooping the Colour a celebration held each year to mark the Queen's birthday

Further information

Books to read:

A Royal Childhood: 200 Years of Royal Babies by Liz Gogerly, Franklin Watts, 2017

All about the Commonwealth by Anita Ganeri, Franklin Watts, 2016.

Queen Elizabeth II: Her Story by John Malam, Wayland 2016.

Queen Elizabeth's Britain by Jacqui Bailey, Franklin Watts, 2015

Real Life Stories: Kate, Duchess of Cambridge by Hettie Bingham, Wayland 2017

The Story of England by Richard Brassey, Orion Children's Books, 2016.

Websites to visit:

Heads Together: the charity set up by the Duke and Duchess of Cambridge and Prince Harry to raise awareness and support for mental health issues and mental wellbeing. *www.headstogether.org.uk*

The **official website of the royal family** has pages on Prince William and Kate. *www.royal.uk*

The **Duke and Duchess of Cambridge have their own website** with information on the many charities and organisations they support: *www.dukeandduchessofcambridge.org*

This page is full of **information about the kings and queens of England**: *www.englishmonarchs.co.uk*

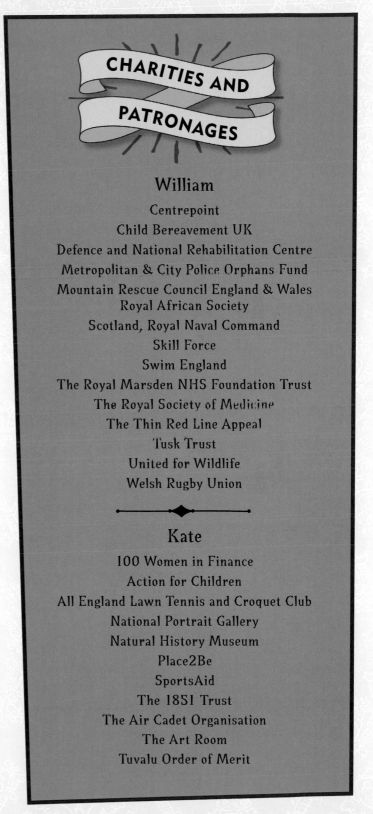

CHARITIES AND PATRONAGES

William

Centrepoint
Child Bereavement UK
Defence and National Rehabilitation Centre
Metropolitan & City Police Orphans Fund
Mountain Rescue Council England & Wales
Royal African Society
Scotland, Royal Naval Command
Skill Force
Swim England
The Royal Marsden NHS Foundation Trust
The Royal Society of Medicine
The Thin Red Line Appeal
Tusk Trust
United for Wildlife
Welsh Rugby Union

Kate

100 Women in Finance
Action for Children
All England Lawn Tennis and Croquet Club
National Portrait Gallery
Natural History Museum
Place2Be
SportsAid
The 1851 Trust
The Air Cadet Organisation
The Art Room
Tuvalu Order of Merit

Index